Continuity Errors

Continuity Errors

CATRIONA WRIGHT

COACH HOUSE BOOKS, TORONTO

first edition

 Canada Council **Conseil des Arts**
for the Arts du Canada

 ONTARIO ARTS COUNCIL
CONSEIL DES ARTS DE L'ONTARIO
an Ontario government agency
un organisme du gouvernement de l'Ontario

Canadä

Published with the generous assistance of the Canada Council for the Arts
and the Ontario Arts Council. Coach House Books also acknowledges the
support of the Government of Canada through the Canada Book Fund and
the Government of Ontario through the Ontario Book Publishing Tax Credit.

LIBRARY AND ARCHIVES CANADA CATALOGUING IN PUBLICATION

Title: Continuity errors / Catriona Wright.
Names: Wright, Catriona, author.
Description: Poems.
Identifiers: Canadiana (print) 20220465908 | Canadiana (ebook)
20220465924 | ISBN 9781552454596 (softcover) | ISBN 9781770567511
(EPUB) | ISBN 9781770567528 (PDF)
Classification: LCC PS8645.R5188 C66 2023 | DDC C811/.6—dc23

Continuity Errors is available as an ebook: ISBN 978 1 77056 751 1 (EPUB),
ISBN 978 1 77056 752 8 (PDF)

CONTENTS

III.

For Rowan

'Every day with a child, I have discovered, is a kind of time travel. I cast my mind ahead with each decision I make, wondering what I might be giving or taking from my child in the future.'

– Eula Biss

CONTINUITY

bullet holes dot the wall
hours before the big shootout

the glass of pink lemonade
replenishes with every sip

the postman's mole
roves his stubbled face

these errors are so common
it should be no surprise when

the dying ash in our yard
bursts into cherry blossoms

our apartment is on Bloor
when it isn't on Bathurst

I laugh and my hair is a bob
I nod into a blond pixie

the baby we didn't have
throws mashed squash on the floor

we flicker between possibilities,
mourn, are reborn over and over

I clean pale vomit off the tiles,
first teal, then desert blush

in the final cut, our lives, sputtering
and contrary, already vaster than us

I.

NOTES TOWARD AN ANTHROPOCENE
FABLE AT A RUSSIAN SAUNA
IN MISSISSAUGA

Rumpelstiltskin's first wife, I enter and exit
the steam room in a eucalyptus cloud.
My rumpled robe scratches. Silt rises

to skin. I scrub my pores with sea salt.
I pull a rusted chain, and a wooden bucket tips
cool torrent on my head.

No one in these microclimates has a name
big enough for forests, for air.
I am trying to outrun my recurring

daymare, the one with the turret.
This olive string bikini, once sinuous,
is now fit only for sweat.

I beg a regular in a wool cap
to wave his parched birch wand.
My inner bitch wakes up, whining.

I haven't fed her in too long.
My cells realign themselves, spread
around. I eavesdrop on the heat,

practise different pronunciations. He ate,
she ate, we all ate the sun's treats,
licked black seeds from slit vanilla beans,

plucked gold croaks from toad throats.
I am trying to escape the king's wealth,
the kind that slashes and slinks through ozone.

I get to stay here longer than the white rhinos,
the bees. Will I hand a first-born to the burn?
Infused with cedar scent, buzzing, I lower

myself into a barrel of glacial water.
I imagine a cryogenic Prince Charming
carrying me, limp, into the next ice age.

Soothed, I shower. Calmer and slower, I sit
in the tea room afterward, drinking
vodka and kombucha, replenishing

my microbiome with pickle brine.
A television displays our ever after,
those fabulous coral bows and rainbows

frozen white in the sunshine.

WINGS

I got them removed.

They bunched up under blazers.
At the beach, people stared.

I had to sit on chairs backwards
like a teacher trying to relate.

Most doctors don't believe in them
and the few that do warn of inflammation.

My aunt's got so rowdy
they flapped her up and out

of her job, her marriage,
a life organized

around wealth.
I'm happier without them,

I think, though I will miss
the wind's rough hands

smoothing my feathers,
how from certain angles I looked

like my grandmother.

CRYPTID CAPTIVE BREEDING PROGRAM

They fly us around the world in reinforced tanks,
stick us together in a canal so narrow
we can't pass each other without touching,
flipper to fin, gill to skin. They play Marvin Gaye
through underwater speakers and light up the sky
with volcanic fireworks. What do they know about love,
these horny gawkers tossing oysters at our heads?

We awoke spontaneously in lake muck, stunned
and lonely, motherless. Even if we wanted to mate,
we fear our lack of parental models has fucked us up,
made us disorganized in our attachments,
needy. Back home I rebuffed the kind lamprey
and clung to the speckled trout who hated me.
I know so little about how to live
a good life or about who I want to be.

It's been a week now and we've stayed
at our respective ends of the canal.
I don't know who is supposed to make
the first move. I don't know what goes where.
I don't know if I'm the one who lays the eggs
or the one who presses cold compresses
on the egg-layer's lower back, guiltily
whispering encouragement.

ROUTINE

My husband reads aloud
an article about embodied presence
in virtual environments.

I take my body, or whatever
you want to call this, on its evening
constitutional to the fridge.

The Chardonnay box's finicky
plastic nipple leaks,
drips cold, oaked relief.

Floating, I soak lima beans,
imagine them reconstituting slowly, plumping
in the dark, never quite themselves.

LOVERS' RETREAT

At the only pub in town, a bartender serves us
lager (flat) and jellied eels (rancid) as he narrates
his aquarist career, that one time an octopus
suctioned to his face, in love, lustfully

pulsing. Reverent, he describes the ridges in her
mantle, submission, how her skin took on
his freckles and blush. Drunk, flushed, we
can feel our own faces speckled

with intricate hickeys. We settle up, stumble
back to the guest house, panting, pausing long enough
to observe the slugs. The road seething
with them. Ribbed nightmares

with green gunk oozing out of holes. We blink
and they become petals: tender, sentient,
pulsating. We follow along, careful
to avoid killing them,

holding hands for the first time in months.

THE ISLAND

I.

Glacial erratics carpeted in ghost moss
and muted blue lichen guarded
the island where I lived to forage
contortions of fungus and extract
their essence for tinctures. Luckily I was born
with scabbed orange hands, dirt-lined
and callused, sturdy and thick-knuckled.

II.

In July, my employer would visit with his ledger
and his hay-lined crates and blocks of ice
to take my potions to the mainland.
He was a man who loved me best
with a shaved head and blisters and boils
bursting white pus. He felt safe around ugliness
and could enjoy the rugged beauty of the island
in peace. Nine months after my employer rowed away
I gave birth.

III.

That first return I hid her from my employer.
She slept, curling and uncurling her fists, quietly
sighing, in a chest beneath my bed.
My employer ignored the thick sweet milk
engorging my lopsided breasts. He approved
of the red stretch marks criss-crossing my stomach
but seemed wary of the smiles I couldn't suppress.
He scribbled inventory lists in his leather ledger,
secured the tinctures, beat me, left.

IV.

The baby, rosy and smooth, bouncing
among the ferns, was too beautiful to be safe.
I scratched her with blunted nails and cut
her cheeks with a rusty blade. Scars rose
symmetrical and shining. She looked stitched
together with moonlight. I broke her legs.
I starved her. She floated through the forest
of bent pines and warped oaks. Seagulls
brought her boughs laden with blueberries.
Her bones healed.

V.

I wept and caressed her, laying her to rest
on craggy granite, winds her swaddling
blankets. She shouted at the sky, thriving,
stronger and sweeter and more vulnerable every day.
My employer returned. I hid her in a damp cave
and begged her to shush, but he soon heard her
burbling, understood her loveliness,
and with the crates and ice
and tinctures, my employer took her away.

DEPOSITION

At the corporate retreats
we invited our employees
to spend time in the coffin.

We didn't cheap out either,
it wasn't some pine box. A modern coffin
with a little pillow inside, satin-lined.

You would have liked it.
You would have liked to rest in it
and feel untouchably rich.

The employee in question would lie
in the coffin and listen while we listed
their flaws. A purifying choir.

It was good for them. Difficult but good
to confront how they'd sabotaged
success, failed themselves and us.

We wanted them to accept
their limitless potential. As you know,
things get in the way: fear, family, rest.

If the coffin didn't work, we tied them to
the cross, mahogany, polished,
you could see your reflection, winking.

We tied them to the cross in the normal way.
They hold their arms and legs still.
You tighten the knots.

DATE NIGHT

Some of my friends are drinking
and placing their feet in bags of acid.
Others are chanting and rolling rose
quartz on their cheeks or snorting
collagen pills to make their hair silky.

We are preparing ourselves, each
with our palettes and poisons,
for an evening with our demons.
They like us smooth and confused.
We like them smirking and cruel.

Our demons! They'll arrive on palanquins
of lacquered money. In a cloud
of sweet smoke. Our demons! Impossibly
dapper with pedicured hooves,
tails ending in tufts of hops,

exquisite horns. In certain lights the demons
look like our mothers. In others, our exes
at their shiniest. Our bosses and professors
are in there, too. They'll condescend
and lecture and harangue, activating

shames from childhood we don't want
to escape. This time will be different.
We've asked the moon for guidance.
We've visualized a life without them.

They'll be here any minute
to kiss our exfoliated feet
and extemporize about the erotic
dimensions of power.

This time I'll say something devastating
to shut them up. I swear. How do I look?

PARTY ON

At all the parties now we party
stressed, plotting exit strategies

from that ick, ourselves,
rooms with their sick bays

of succulents, this city
with its sadistic improvisations.

The landlord is moving his dandruff
back in, *yes and*, you have one week

to land on your feet,
yes and, congratulations

on that sessional contract, *yes and*,
understand low demand this semester

means no compensation, *yes and*,
better luck next reincarnation,

yes and, it helps to think of debt
as radical financial vulnerability, *yes*

and, I hear these gigs are a handy
stop gap, *yes and*, some

of the men aren't even that
bad, *yes and*, you are paid

in off-brand cryptocurrency
to feel them breathing

by your ear while you assemble
a bassinet with a warped Allen key,

yes and, you had such grand plans,
didn't you, *yes and*, aren't you bitches

to blame for this impotence
with your plots to unman us,

to siphon testosterone
from our gonads, *yes and*, don't kid

yourself, love has always been
transactional, *yes and*, surge pricing

is inevitable, *and yes*,
stress is an acceptance

of your position, a lesson,
a lessening, a lesion, a loan

your body is not yet authorized to forgive.

THE ORCHID'S LAST WILTING

For millennia
I refined

my interpretation
of the female

bee's genitalia,
my petals subtle

smut not strictly
representational,

playful erotic
abstractions

that don't pander
or lapse into boring

pornography
unlike the work

of some of my
contemporaries.

My loose painterly
style and organic

composition drew
praise and recognition,

pleased my doting
pollinators

who circled and
circled and

landed, ecstatic,
at my openings.

I never wanted
to be a memorial,

an artifact,
a designated mourner,

the last wilting
evidence

of an extinct
bee's exquisite

taste.

I WAS BORN ON A DEAD-END STREET.

My bedroom window faced a brick wall.
From my brother's you could see
the carnival, those Ferris wheel spokes
loud with orange lights. I was stuck
with the bricks and their boring
secrets. They were terrible best friends.

To escape the wall, I visited the junk heap
with its choir of rust. To get there
you had to sprint down a sloping path
bordered with broken daisies while repeating
(silently, silently) the mantra of your secret name.
Mine was High Priestess of Jacked Biceps.
(I trust you with it and anyway I already changed it.)

One day I decided to speak. I lifted our house
and dropped it on an even shorter, deader
street. Now my window faced the end
of the world (my brother's still faced a carnival).
Best friend, keep this between us: in the finale
the sun swallows us but in a fun way, we laugh through
our dying so hard and longer, so softest and bent,
        it never ends

SURRENDER

Cornfield, reveal
contact coordinates.

Clouds, part.
Tractor beam,

paralyze me gently
in your cold light.

I'm ready.
I'm so ready to board

that radiant saucer,
to have my frail

hominid husk shucked
from my true form:

eyes revelling in
infrared, antennae

swishing ecstatically,
my exoskeleton humming

its birth song
as my mind logs on

to a sublime
consciousness

that resolves glitches,
old spluttering hurts,

debugs self-
sabotaging code,

holds me
until I fall asleep.

Tractor beam, whenever
you're ready.

Clouds, please part
me from residual fear.

Cornfield, leave
no trace of my exit.

II.

WAITING ROOM

Before we enter, they take our temperature
and slather our hands in stinging goo.
We are instructed to stay away from each other.
We could wink or raise our eyebrows but don't.
The technicians will be here soon to escort us
to our cubicles and slather more goo, colder,
more viscous, onto our stomachs and use wands
to locate other bodies in our bodies.

The walls are off-white, surprisingly dingy.
Faint handprints on window and door frames,
near escapes. The temperature is kept low
and the chairs uncomfortable so we remain alert
and aloof. Drowsiness breaches the boundaries
that keep us safe. All of us are playgrounds
for other bodies. Boundaries are a joke.

The television, on mute, a commercial.
A mother loads a washer with grass-stained shirts
and muddy socks. She pours in detergent.
The colours must be off. The liquid
should be a vivacious green or blue,
but it's red, deep and treacly, dense,
unending. I need to staunch it badly,
approach the television. The other bodies

tense, like gazelles, which I resent.
I'm not the predator here. I feel possessive of fear,
want to inhabit it, alone, as I'll never be again.
But I make room for them. These women
can't control what their bodies get up to,
not only inviting other bodies in
but offering them warm blankets, bladders
as cushions. I return to my assigned area and close
my eyes to keep the wrong colours out.

Two years ago I sat in this room with a friend.
You could do that kind of thing back then.
Her new body seemed virtuous. The television
played sitcom reruns from the nineties, the colours
vivid and easy. Very special episodes
about eating disorders, drug abuse, unwanted pregnancies,
all resolved by heart-to-hearts and hugs.
A 1-800 hotline for the rest of us.

A technician calls my name. Again, again.
Are you here. Are you here. Are you here.

INNOVATION

In the classroom students are imagining screens
that feel like silk, like silt, fiery as kilns,

off kilter. They discuss a future of stone walls that dissolve
into fog and reconstitute as universal organs, pulsing,

of robot spouses who know when to cuddle
and when coffee and when cancer ceases being

hypochondria. Cantilever bridges alive
with concrete that can heal itself before collapse.

Algorithms to predict crime and epidemics.
In the classroom students are imagining a future

so immaculate they omit turnips, dirt, tantrums, long
aimless walks, lust. They trust the relentless process,

sprint past the prototypes twitching
in their mass graves, last words a slur

of diminishing whirs and forlorn bleeps. Onward!
They forget to eat, and when the tears

splash onto control, delete, they try goggles
until the lenses fill with lacrimal fluid.

They try bigger goggles. Perhaps two sponges
tamping ducts? Tiny drones

to slurp up obsolete secretions? It's a simple matter
of separating mass: keyboard from human weakness.

Can they imagine doubting this new disposition?
Losing faith? To stall, stop, step back.

Imagine watching a chameleon turn magenta
then chartreuse without itching to optimize its magic,

augment its pigments. To be content
having changed nothing in the world

except the way they and their kin stumble through it.

SEASONAL AFFECTIVE DISORDER

I answer winter with Florida,
Blue Moon beermosas, swamp
pontoon rides, fishy pelican breath.
As good a place as any
to drink myself to death.

Clouds piss themselves,
rain slamming mint and lilac
motels, palms, plastic
surgery billboards asking,
Are your cups half empty?

Fearing falling coconuts, I pull over
and watch two gators make
minimalistic love in a ditch. I imagine
my skin thickening to gator hide.
As good a gamble as any
to make my life continuous

prologue. Hibiscus open their dull
fuchsia throats to the humidity.
Hungover, I eat cold noodles
out of a Styrofoam clam,
stroll on damp, gritty sand,
picturing the melancholy
and mystical sex lives inside

the rainbow sherbet houses
precarious on stilts.

Veering between the drunks
blasting beer-and-truck country
and the drunker drunks
blasting breakup country, I step
on something sharp. A clamshell,
or part of one. Ridged blush, cream,
orange, tinged with blood.
A sunset. Good as any.

ULTRAHYDROPHOBICITY

A new material to mimic
the dense papillae peaks

that nanodot the lotus leaf
to keep rain at a distance,

contained in droplets like crystal
balls in which we glimpse

novel future applications,
e.g., margarita-proof

electronics, corrosion-free
metals, neural implant

marvels, oopsy-daisy oil spills,
blood and tears thrown

at a CEO instantly repelled,
transformed into innocuous

red pellets, dry cinnamon
drops bouncing shyly off

his suit, almost admirable
the way that white shirt

stays starched cold,
that slim-fit jacket

still the shameless
cobalt of the self-cleaning

tiles in the largest of his
many several infinity

pools bordering and mocking
the sea.

SUBJECT: MONEY IS DORMANT WITHIN YOU ! ALL AROUND YOU THE UNIVERSE PULSES WITH IT !

congratulations

you've inherited ! a wormhole !
claim rightful pilgrim revenue ! everyone worships !
a spacetime ! tunnel and its pastor !
grateful disciples will spangle ! and lavish ! and wail !
for the first year only yes !
prestige ! epiphanies ! purpose !

falling in love ! with a constellation !
sprouting a star-shaped crown !
you'll finally be you ! only easier and indigo !
in plush prosperity robes ! yes !
the wormhole will whisk ! away ! your heart loans !

envision holy residue ! cosmic self-determination !
for you a clone ! cyclic youth ! a buffet of futures !
why not a moat ! filled with melted bodies !
to deliver that extra oomph ! of divinity !

for drastic results ! mass marry !
yes! limited-edition moons !

act soon

FOUR DREAMS OF ELIZABETH HOLMES

after Will Harris

I.

Once, I removed
my black turtleneck
to reveal another
black turtleneck,
underneath which
another black turtleneck.
Another black turtleneck.
Another. Black turtlenecks.
Black turtlenecks
all the way down.

II.

Once, I rappelled down
the side of an apple,
crampons leaving
delicate pricks
in the waxy red surface.
I could hear the juice
escaping, going
from soprano to baritone,
the holes oxidizing.
Whoever ate the apple
probably didn't notice,
respected the apple more
without knowing why.

III.

Once, I squatted onstage and gave birth
to swirling ash. I was pushed into the wings
as the ash swirled harder and arranged itself
into my loose, smoky daughter. She followed me
home. I was the only one who recognized her.
She had my frizzy hair. My shape-shifting.
The daycares I applied for cited shortages,
fears of lung cancer. I kept her,
condensed, in a Thermos on my desk
and let her out for meetings with investors.

IV.

Once, I was red wax
dripping onto an envelope,
pressed into a seal.
I kept the secrets
until a heat wave
weakened my charisma.
No one was safe.

TRUST FUND

The medium is lying to me. She claims to have channelled Cleopatra and Aleister Crowley. When presenting an invoice, she insists she used her mystical capital to lobby on my behalf with visionaries and oracles. Yet the voices she brings back are stale, static, none of that pure fire energy I need to ignite the life I sense within me. Erotic epiphanies and spiritual intrigue. Transcendence. An instant classic. I hired the medium as a shortcut, a scout to send into the underworld in search of fresh red seeds and spirits. The dead know how to live. Money has been my only ally. My parents spoke in dividends. Please understand I'm generous, I tip well, I'm grateful to have been born with enough money to solve problems, remove discomforts, except this persistent cowardice, my sweat soaking through the duvet. My medium is lying to me. It is the only love I recognize. My inbox is a world of lures, swaying. She isn't the first. She isn't the first to see what I am. I place my fingers on the planchette and beg to make contact.

SCAMMER

after Eiléan Ní Chuilleanáin

When all this is over, said the scammer,
I'm going to retire to a seaside village
within pissing distance of a starfish.
I pray old age makes me oblivious.

I want to see a rich widow weeping
without feeling that delicious itch.
I'll just sip my lager and smile along
while the locals bitch about tourists.

I won't sell the acne-prone fishmonger
a miracle serum. I won't cry shark.
I'll collect sand dollars with the vicar,
letting him keep the very best ones.

SPECIES LONELINESS

Like everyone else, I use trees
as a metaphor for myself
and my dream community.

The way they share sugar, party
with mushrooms, lean on each other, learn
not to binge on soil moisture in spring.

They even scream ultrasonically! From thirst.
I am not above anthropomorphizing trees.
I can't think as plants think

though maybe in future I will
hire a tree sensitivity reader
who will delicately point out how wrong I am

about everything. I welcome this as I welcome all
(okay, most!) confirmations of my ignorance.
Make my trunk stronger, thicker, more receptive.

Trees know what they have to do
and they get on with it. They throw shade, they turn
red and yellow for a few weeks then sleep, they toss

and drop and gussy up their seeds, they are full
of busy holes. Who doesn't want
to be like that? I suspect they wouldn't be wild

about being compared to me, given how bent
I've grown, how straggled my crown, how I gorge
on nutrients only to throw them back up,

how my roots took a decade-long smoke break
after barely nudging into soil, how I blossom out of sync
with my neighbours, how I never even bothered

to learn their names.

DANSE BRUTALISTE

after William Carlos Williams

I take ballet lessons in a Brutalist building.
I'm bad at everything except believing
I'm good. In movies this building is a prison
or a tyrant's corporate headquarters.
Secrets are worshipped here. The concrete.
The angles. The crisp shadows.
I dance in a cold room in the suburbs
of conformity. None of my lines are good.
My body squiggles and flops. The teacher sighs,
tells me to suck in my gut. Other girls giggle.

I know that if the torturers appear
with glints and if the henchmen hench
toward me, I'll be ready to menace
them with inelegance. A secret genius
with bad turnout and a sloppy bun
bewildering them with a pirouette
that wobbles but nevertheless
becomes perpetual, perpetual
blur and slip, repeat and whirl,
as likely as anything
to banish loneliness from the world.

MORE SEASONAL AFFECTIVE DISORDER

We answer winter
with more winter
and colder, snow
thicker, days shorter.
Driving north to good
trails, groomed
swerves through groves
of pine and silver birch.
Driving north to hoppy
ales, a wood-burning stove
awakened with iron blow
poke, grey embers throbbing
orange, releasing sweet
smoke. We haven't awakened
anything this year or not
that thing I wanted most.
Someone to keep warm
with these rainbow mittens,
this nubby woollen hat
with earflaps tied under chin.
Someone to wobble into
that sparkling white field,
follow those hoofprints,
heart-shaped, disappearing
fast beneath clotting flakes.

III.

WAKE AT THE TIKI BAR

Our only light
a blowfish

blown up,
pale yellow

afterlife glowing
through spiky skin.

Someone rings
a gong, splits

the silence.
Who hallucinated

this place?
On the wall, carved

masks grimace,
displaced

deities.
Thatched awning

over the bar,
bamboo, rattan,

some dead
American's fever

dream of escape.
Loose in time,

we are served
a fishbowl

of booze, flaming
lime as garnish.

The smell of charred
pineapple

and rum, memories
of stealing sips

from a late parent's
liquor cabinet.

We open tiny
brittle parasols,

remember
the cooling

greenish sheen
of aloe vera gel

(the fake kind,
all additives)

on scorched skin,
how simple

it seemed to heal
back then.

We place our
bent straws

into the burn,
rush to absorb

something before
the ice cubes can

dilute our good-
enough oblivions.

THE NUMBER TEN BUS

lists through snow-damp streets.
It hiccups, jolts. Cold air seeps through
sloppily jointed seams. We miss a stop,
then another. Those left behind curse the wake
of slush. I hate it here, stuck, forced
to collaborate on the future. A man
tries to sell me a rose, petals intricate
with aphids, tiny green bodies
forming a shifting embroidery.
Women's work. Risk assessment, selling *no*
as firm yet gentle self-effacement.
Another missed stop. Lice love it here,
all these scalps to redecorate. A toddler
is absorbed into celestial upholstery.
His father, desperate, searches the seat
for an entrance, probing frayed stars
and seams, then pleading with me
for help. Women's work. Compassion
and fabric warp and rematerializing children.
Smiling, I shrug and pull the exit cord.
Over the intercom the driver whispers
my name, coos it in a lullaby voice.
Another missed stop. Another.
Almost there, the driver sings, *almost there,*
you silly sop, for once, just once,
sit still and stop making everything
about you and your unremarkable loss.

SOMEBODY HAD TO DO IT

I wiped the windows until I could see the howl
of static – snow drifting off the sky's dry scalp.
I fed garbage bags old birthday cards
and broken teapots. Coughing, I dragged a rag
through the baseboards' purple dust.
The air filled with cloying orange-scented mist
as if I were entering the dying orchard of her lungs.
Dresses swayed in the closet. I kept the lilac bias-
cut gown and shoved the rest, wailing,
into body bags. All night I scrubbed and swept,
removing sadnesses. The rings in the toilet bowl.
Grey strands snarled in boar bristles. In her study,
an effusion of staked blooms. She liked orchids best
because they thrive on neglect. The floors
creaked, clearing their throats, as if preparing
to deliver a scathing assessment of my progress.
All night I cleaned like someone who believes
in forgiveness, hers or mine. Morning came,
and the snow paused. I wrung the last
sponge into the sink and watched the murk swirl
away, my body loosening with the bliss
of a newborn, freshly burped.

FIFTEEN

I smoked pot in a rhododendron
cathedral by the canal, pink petals
sputtering through thick plumes. I parted
branches and entered the afternoon.
In the canal's radioactive waters
carp thrashed to the surface. We fed
them Pringles and Sour Patch Kids,
bright corpses covered in powdery
down, the first frost. Sour. Sweet. Gone.

That year my two best friends
soured on me. They were gone.
I went begging for new friends.
I made out with a boy who sailed
tall ships in the summer. He had fish
eyes. I fed him lies and ladyfingers
soaked in chocolate milk. He told me
he was born on the same green couch
he was fingering me on. My mother
wanted to know what was wrong,
why I didn't want a birthday party
that year, a cake with buttercream petals.

I made excuses. I made friends
with a girl who snorted PCP off her desk
during physics. Probably just some sour
sugar powder that scorched her nostrils.
She made me friendship bracelets
using pink and green string, her hair,
thousands of tiny intimate knots. I didn't
love her, couldn't unlove my old friends
because they resurfaced, tall and ladyfinger-slim,
in every hallway. They starred
in all the school plays, the sweetest gossip.
Barbed laughter clung to me
as I clanged my locker shut.

Every afternoon I'd climb into
that dim chamber, into that mausoleum
with its perfume of rotting flowers
and rutting skunks, light filtering down
in barbs and lances. I'd get high and resurrect
my imaginary friend, Petite, who I stabbed
with a toy sword when I was six. She sat
cross-legged in the dirt and asked for a hit.
We drank chocolate milk, cracked jokes
and invisible eggs on each other, the yolks
running warm and wayward down our backs.
I'd get a good green hour before she noticed
the flaking gold hilt in her chest.

HOW TO EXPECT: A TRIPTYCH

I. January

Every afternoon I walk through the cemetery.
It's a pleasant cemetery, active
with mourners, bright greenhouse flowers.
Bare oaks sway above.
The crows are cheerful and brave.

I walk through the cemetery
and hope to feel you move inside me.
In ultrasound scans, you are a ghost.
One of those hoax photographs
from the nineteenth century.

When I googled *is it wrong to have a baby?*
the algorithm told me,
*to bear children into this world
is like carrying wood into a burning house.*

A woman crouches by a headstone.
Her finger melts the snow
as she traces or creates
a name.

II. Work

We collaborate
on a new organ,
an interface.
We speak in blood
and waste, pale pleas
between our bodies.
You make coffee
taste metallic. *Placenta*
comes from the Latin
for *honey cake*. Please eat,
little bee, let me
clean the plate.

III. Parallel

When we first met
you were two blue lines

I didn't believe in you yet
I quadruple-checked

Now my body has an unruly allure
but I'm still too shy for nudes

On the fridge a gallery of your body
your toes and upturned nose

Some days I think you're a prank
I'm pulling on my past

We live in parallel realities
You don't believe in me yet

I'm just squishy walls
a loud wet climate

My birth plan is no pain
and the glaciers stop melting

I can't fix the world
before you get here

I hope you like your name

THE LOVE SONG OF DUST

after C. D. Wright

You don't have to deal with me. To lend me
money, to pity-eat my soggy macaroni salad,
to patiently explain some new technology yet again.
I am your ancestor. Maybe you would have liked me?
I never saved for retirement or cared that much
about my liver. In a small garden I planted bee balm
and milkweed for pollinators. I cared about them.
I was a poet of split ends, hangnails, hangovers.
Of digressions and Netflix binges. Of Dorito dust.
I abandoned drafts and conflicts but was a blast
at parties if you caught me early enough.
The future scared me.

I was a poet of pettiness and vanity. I wept
when not nominated, awarded, noticed.
It is ugly to admit and I was often a poet of ugliness.
My ambition far outstripped my talent.
I was a poet of rage-scrolling and procrastination.
On rare occasions, stoned or exhausted,
I grasped how the word *scarcity*
warped and wrung me, then quickly
forgot. All the extra-strength lip balms
at the bottom of my purse dried up.
I returned library books late and took
the pill at a different time each day.

I never met my grandparents, never tamped
their pipes or inhaled their dandruff or heard
versions of my parents' stories. I floated,
insecurely tethered to my lineage: white skin, witticisms,
a predisposition for colon cancer. I am your ancestor.
Do you feel close to me? Do you have my teeth?
The past existed only when I read
the words of the dead. The poets of attentiveness
and confession and joy. It was easy to be expansive
imagining my ghost mingling with theirs.

I was the poet of a single life,
nothing more. No journalists asked
what I was working on next. No university
stored my juvenilia in a special collection.
I'm sorry. You've heard this before.
I stashed my shame under the floorboards
of poems and congratulated myself
on my stealth. Do you still do that?
Or are you healthy? Maybe you brushed me
off your new life, like lint? I wasn't all bad.
Do you still save eggshells and coffee grounds
for the butterfly bush? Laugh too loud? Eavesdrop
too conspicuously? Poet of spit-up epaulettes
and diaper ceremonies. Of dishwasher tablets.
Poet of winter tires and flossing and fibre
and dragging the recycling to the curb.

VIABLE

as of this week
you could survive

weak, reliant on tubes
nevertheless alive

stay inside a little
while longer

how about
forever

kick once for yes
kick once for no

keep our heart
beats steady

lie to me
I'm ready

I PUSHED YOU OUT AND OFFERED MY BREAST,

a champagne coupe of colostrum.
All business, consultants assessed
that first latch, scoring suction, seal,
the fish-mouth flange of your lower lip.

In the days that followed you drank,
and as you drank, the golden liquid
clouded and matured into milk,
tasting sweetly of almonds and cantaloupe.

I leaked through nursing pads, bras.
My blouses all had hidden snaps and flaps
to allow easier access to my aching ducts.
Days of cluster feeding, all-night binges.

My nipples bled, parched and stinging
into a season of prohibition
neither of us had prepared for. An addict,
you pleaded, licked, bargained with my bouncers

to release elixir. At night, you screamed and bit
them, incensed. I ate flax seed and brewer's yeast,
drank stout and blessed thistle tea, convinced
this drought was evidence I'd flunked another

motherhood test no one had warned me about.
I pumped. A sad dribble. I prayed. Your father
funnelled formula into a bottle and lifted
the squat rubber nipple – crude as a Big Gulp

straw – to your lips, I cried with you
as you sucked, delirious, belligerent,
relieved, betrayer and betrayed.

SLEEP-DEPRIVED EEG

Electrodes glued to your scalp
        and cheeks. A connecting rainbow
of wires wrapped in gauze.

I zip you into a cloud
        swaddle and play rainstorm
sounds on my phone. We wait.

Blue and orange squiggles
        appear onscreen, bridges
to your refracted dream

world. I haven't slept,
        not really, since the birth,
my mind a mist lit up

with you. Dispersed, up late, I listen
        to my labour playlist.
Willie Nelson's soft cover of 'The Rainbow

Connection.' In the morning
        I mix you an unholy pink potion
of breast milk and phenobarbital.

Pink doesn't exist in rainbows
        where red and violet never meet.
You smile in your sleep.

I want to cross a bridge into the green
        meadow of your dreams and meet you,
to feel the electrical storm surging through

the indigo sky and the sweet calm after.
        These midnight wishes are answered
with another afternoon like this,

chasing traces and smudges, searching for
        that golden place – a diagnosis.
The doctors say we might never

find it, it might not exist, and in this way
        you are a poem, kaleidoscope
luck, the pinkest morning star.

KEEP THE CHANNEL OPEN

Concentrating, concatenating,
my infant son splices syllables

with white noise, gurgles, word clatter,
the endangered bleeps, clicks, and static

of dial-up internet, the accelerated grind
of an asteroid mine. Listen closely

to the slurped vowels, how he travels
back, an aspiring starling stealing

the great auk's masterful squawk, and is that
the crackle of a needle on vinyl?

He is a medium exuberantly
channelling past and future soundscapes.

A tonsured monk's lacerating Latin confessions.
A replicated sabre-tooth's cybernetic roar.

Let him stay this way as long as he can, fluent
in every noise, necrolinguist, xenosong futurist,

crying with all the decibel-force of the Big Bang
and its gulping, bungled burst.

NOTES

The epigraph is from Eula Biss's *On Immunity: An Inoculation* (Graywolf Press, 2014).

p. 26: 'Deposition' is inspired by the episode 'The Mind Is a Fertile Field' from the podcast *The Dream*, hosted by Jane Marie and Dann Gallucci. In this episode, they discuss the history of the multi-level marketing industry, including the legacy of William Penn Patrick, an entrepreneur who ran a 'leadership' training program during which participants were placed in coffins and tied to crosses.

p. 32: 'The Orchid's Last Wilting' is indebted to Donna Haraway's *Staying with the Trouble: Making Kin in the Chthulucene* (Duke University Press, 2016).

p. 48: Elizabeth Holmes is the founder of Theranos, a biotechnology company that claimed to have developed revolutionary blood-testing technology, which was later proven to be fraudulent. She raised more than $700 million from private investors and venture capitalists. In 2022, she was convicted of criminal fraud and conspiracy.

p. 80: The title 'Keep the Channel Open' comes from an interview with Martha Graham that appears in *Martha: The Life and Work of Martha Graham* by Agnes de Mille (Random House, 1991).

ACKNOWLEDGEMENTS

Poems from this collection have previously appeared in the *Walrus, This Magazine, Humber Literary Review, Dalhousie Review, Prism International, Magma* (U.K.), and the *American Poetry Review*. Thank you to the editors.

Thank you to the Toronto Arts Council, the Ontario Arts Council, and the Canada Council for the Arts for providing vital support during the writing of this book.

Thank you to Myra Bloom, Aaron Kreuter, and Michael Prior for reading earlier drafts of this manuscript and providing valuable feedback. Thank you to all the members of Mark Waldron's poetry workshop, run through the Poetry School (U.K.), for their intelligent suggestions and good humour.

It has been a joy and an honour to work with Coach House Books. I am grateful to Matthew Tierney for his perceptive editing, to Crystal Sikma for the gorgeous cover, and to Alana Wilcox and James Lindsay for their dedication, enthusiasm, and support.

Thank you, finally, to my husband, Ted, for encouraging me to write through the pandemic and pregnancy, and to my son, Rowan, for re-enchanting the world.

Catriona Wright is the author of the poetry collection *Table Manners* and the short story collection *Difficult People.* Her poems have appeared in the *American Poetry Review,* the *Walrus,* and *Magma,* and they have been anthologized in *The Next Wave: An Anthology of 21st Century Canadian Poetry* and in *Best Canadian Poetry* 2015 and 2018.

Typeset in Arno and Quiche Text.

Printed at the Coach House on bpNichol Lane in Toronto, Ontario, on Zephyr Antique Laid paper, which was manufactured, acid-free, in Saint-Jérôme, Quebec, from second-growth forests. This book was printed with vegetable-based ink on a 1973 Heidelberg KORD offset litho press. Its pages were folded on a Baumfolder, gathered by hand, bound on a Sulby Auto-Minabinda, and trimmed on a Polar single-knife cutter.

Coach House is on the traditional territory of many nations, including the Mississaugas of the Credit, the Anishnabeg, the Chippewa, the Haudenosaunee, and the Wendat peoples, and is now home to many diverse First Nations, Inuit, and Métis peoples. We acknowledge that Toronto is covered by Treaty 13 with the Mississaugas of the Credit. We are grateful to live and work on this land.

Edited by Matthew Tierney
Cover design by Crystal Sikma, cover art *Mulher Na Cadeira Verde* by
   Tania Costa
Interior design by Crystal Sikma
Author photo by Eric Overton

Coach House Books
80 bpNichol Lane
Toronto ON M5S 3J4
Canada

416 979 2217
800 367 6360

mail@chbooks.com
www.chbooks.com